COOL JOBS
for
Yard-Working Kids

Ways to Make Money
Doing Yard Work

Pam Scheunemann

ABDO
Publishing Company

Visit us at www.abdopublishing.com

Published by ABDO Publishing Company, 8000 West 78th Street, Edina, Minnesota 55439.
Copyright © 2011 by Abdo Consulting Group, Inc. International copyrights reserved in all countries.
No part of this book may be reproduced in any form without written permission from the publisher.
The Checkerboard Library™ is a trademark and logo of ABDO Publishing Company.

Printed in the United States , North Mankato, Minnesota
052010
092010

 PRINTED ON RECYCLED PAPER

Design and Production: Kelly Doudna, Mighty Media, Inc.
Series Editor: Liz Salzmann
Photo Credits: Kelly Doudna, Fotolia, iStockPhoto (Bonnie Jacobs, Don Nichols, ImageInnovation Photography, Lawrence Sawyer, Steve Stone), Shutterstock
Money Savvy Pig® photo courtesy of Money Savvy Generation/www.msgen.com

**Library of Congress
Cataloging-in-Publication Data**

Scheunemann, Pam, 1955-
  Cool jobs for yard-working kids : ways to make money doing yard work / Pam Scheunemann.
    p. cm. -- (Cool kid jobs)
  Includes index.
  ISBN 978-1-61613-198-2
  1. Money-making projects for children--Juvenile literature.
2. Gardening--Vocational guidance--Juvenile literature. 3. Success in business--Juvenile literature. 4. Finance, Personal --Juvenile literature. I. Title.
  HF5392.S343 2011
  635.9'64023--dc22
                    2010004317

NOTE TO ADULTS

A job can be a good learning experience for you and your child. Be sure to encourage your child to discuss his or her job ideas with you. Talk about the risks and the benefits. Set up some rules for your child's safety with regard to:

* working with strangers

* transportation to and from the job

* proper and safe use of tools or equipment

* giving out phone numbers or e-mail addresses

* emergency contacts

Contents

Why Work? 4

What Can You Do with Your Money? 5

What's Your Plan? 6

Get Permission 8

Be Smart, Be Safe 9

Getting the Word Out 10

Money Matters 14

Pro Mow Lawn Service 16

Leaf the Raking to Me 18

Weeds Be Gone 20

Let It Snow Shoveling Service 22

Clean Yard, Happy Yard 24

Thirsty Plant Watering Service 26

For the Birds 28

Tips for Success 30

This Is Just the Beginning 30

Glossary 31

Web Sites 31

Index 32

Why Work?

There are a lot of reasons to have a job. The first one you probably think of is to earn money. But you can get more out of a job than just money. You can learn new skills, meet new people, and get some experience.

MAKING MONEY

When you do a job such as raking leaves or shoveling snow, you are providing a service. If people pay you for your service, you can earn some money!

BESIDES MONEY

You will gain more than money from having a job. You also get work experience and learn about being responsible. That means showing up on time, keeping your word, and being trustworthy.

Volunteering is doing a job you don't get paid for. But you can earn other rewards. You can learn new skills that will help you get other jobs. And you can feel good about helping out!

What Can You Do with Your Money?

There are four things you can do with the money you earn.

SAVE

Saving is keeping your money in a safe place. You add money a little at a time as you earn it. Soon you could save enough for something such as a new bike.

SPEND

Spending is using your money to buy things you want. Maybe you want to go to a movie or buy a new computer game.

DONATE

It is important to give some of your earnings to organizations that help others.

INVEST

Investing is saving for long-term goals such as college expenses.

Ask your parents to help you decide how much money to use for each purpose. You'll be glad you did!

Money Savvy Pig®

What's Your Plan?

Each state has laws about kids working. If you are too young to work at a regular job, you can create your own job. Whatever job you try, you should have a plan.

WHAT WILL YOU DO?

Your job should relate to your abilities and likes. Make a list of the kinds of outdoor work you know how to do. Which do you like doing the most? That's a good place to start!

WHO ARE YOUR CUSTOMERS?

Who needs your product or service? Where will you find your customers? How will you let people know about your services?

WHERE WILL YOU DO THE WORK?

Will you work at your house, the customers' homes, or another location?

SETTING REALISTIC GOALS

A goal is something you are working toward. When you set your job goals, keep these questions in mind:

* Do you have permission from your parents?

* Is your idea something you already know how to do?

* Will this job interfere with your schoolwork or other activities?

* Are there any costs to start your job? Do you have the money, or do you need to get a loan?

* Are there tools or **materials** you need to start your job? Will you continue to need supplies?

* Will you work alone or with a friend? How will you divide the work and the money you make?

What If It Doesn't Work?

Don't get **discouraged** if things don't work out the way you planned. Think about what you could have done differently and try again!

Get Permission

You must get permission from a parent or **guardian** before you work for someone else. Give your parents all of the details about the job.

WHO WILL YOU BE WORKING FOR?

Are you working for a relative or friend of the family? If not, your parents should meet your customer.

WHEN WILL YOU BE WORKING?

What day will you start the work? What time? Will your services be needed once or more often?

WHERE IS THE JOB?

Be sure your family has the address and phone number of where you are working. Create a Customer Information form similar to the one on page 15. Fill out a form for each customer.

HOW WILL YOU GET THERE?

Is your job within walking or biking distance? Do you need a ride there? Is it okay for you to take the bus to get there? What if it's during the evening or after dark?

WHO ELSE WILL BE THERE?

Are you going to do the job alone or with a friend? Will there be other people around while you are working?

WHAT IS EXPECTED OF YOU?

Are you clear about the job you were hired to do? Have you made an agreement with the customer about what is expected of you (see page 14)?

Be Smart, Be Safe

Talk with your parents about working for strangers. Always tell your parents where you are going and what time they should expect you to be home. Make sure they have a phone number where they can reach you while you are working.

YARD WORK SAFETY

It is important to be sure you know how to use the tools for yard work. Be careful when using sharp tools. Stretch a bit before you start doing a lot of **physical** work. Learn the proper way to lift a shovel or other heavy objects. Know about poisonous weeds—you don't want to end up with poison ivy!

Work gloves are a must for most of the jobs in this book. Make sure you have permission to use power tools such as lawn mowers or edgers.

Getting the Word Out

Okay, you've decided what to do. Now how do you get the work? There are different ways to get the word out.

BUSINESS CARDS

A simple business card can be very helpful in getting customers. Give cards to the people you talk to about your business. Maybe even give each person an extra so he or she can pass one along to a friend.

Your business card should have your name, your business name, and your phone number. Get permission from a parent before putting your home address, phone number, or e-mail address on a card.

WORD OF MOUTH

Let as many people know about your business as you can. They'll tell other people, and those people will tell more people, and so on.

Make Your Own Business Cards

Pro Mow Lawn Service

Rebecca Jones
123 Address Drive
Dearborn, MI 48126
(313) 555-0139

PRO TIP
Use the computer to make your flyer and cards. Or, follow the steps here and on page 13 for a more personal touch.

1. On a piece of white paper, draw a rectangle with a black pen. It should be 3½ x 2 inches (9 x 5 cm). Design your business card inside the rectangle.

2. Make 11 copies of the card. Cut each one out, including the original. Cut outside the border so the lines show.

3. Tape the cards onto a piece of 8½ x 11-inch (22 x 28 cm) paper. Leave a ¼-inch (½ cm) border around the edge of the paper. This is your business card **master**.

4. Copy the master onto card stock. If you're using a black-and-white copier, try using colored card stock. Or, use white card stock and add color with markers or colored pencils.

5. Cut out your business cards. When you run out of cards, make more copies of your master.

WHAT YOU'LL NEED

white paper	tape
ruler	card stock (white or colored)
black pen	
copier	markers or colored pencils
scissors	

Pro Mow Lawn Service

Do you need reliable lawn services?

* Grass Mowing
* Leaf Raking
* Garden Care
* Bird Feeding
* Snow Shoveling

Pro Mow Lawn Service can help!
* Experienced in lawn care
* Reasonable rates
Call Rebecca Jones for an estimate
(313) 555-0139

Pro Mow Lawn Service
(333) 555-0139

A flyer is a one-page sheet about your product or service. You can include more information than will fit on a business card. Make little mini cards at the bottom of the flyer for people to tear off. Include your service and phone number. Get your parent's permission first! Give flyers to people you know. Also, some places have bulletin boards for flyers:

* stores
* community centers
* schools
* places of worship

Make Your Own Flyer

1 Design a **master** copy of your flyer on a sheet of white paper that is 8½ x 11 inches (22 x 28 cm).

2 Use bright colors so your flyer will stand out. If you plan to use a black-and-white copier, use black on the master, and copy it onto colored paper.

3 Remember that copiers won't copy anything written too close to the edge of the master. So leave a white border on all sides.

4 Make as many copies of the master as you need. Cut the lines between the mini cards so customers can tear them off easily.

WHAT YOU'LL NEED

white paper

black pen

ruler

markers or colored pencils

copier

colored paper (optional)

scissors

Money Matters

One reason to work is so you can make money!

Here are some hints about money.

Sample form: make yours fit your business!

❀ Pro Mow Customer Agreement

Customer Name _____
Address _____
_____
Phone _____
Job Description _____
_____
Start Date _____ End Date _____

❀ Schedule

MONDAY	TUESDAY	WEDNESDAY	THURSDAY	FRIDAY	SATURDAY	SUNDAY

❀ Rate/Payment Agreement

Customer agrees to pay Pro Mow Lawn Service $_____
for the services listed above in the job description for each
(hour, day, week, month).

Payments will be made on a (per visit, weekly, monthly) basis.

_____   _____
Customer Signature   Date

Pro Mow Lawn Service
Rebecca Jones, 123 Address Drive, Dearborn, MI 48126
(313) 555-0139

HOW MUCH SHOULD YOU CHARGE?

Here are things to consider when figuring out what to charge.

* Find out what other people charge for the same product or service.

* Are you providing tools or supplies? Make sure you charge enough to cover your costs.

* Do you want to charge by the hour or by the job? Will you charge less if they are steady customers?

MAKE AN AGREEMENT

Be clear with your customer about how much you are charging. Discuss the details with the customer.

Pro Mow Customer Information

Customer:	
Address:	
Phone Number:	
Emergency Phone Numbers:	
Owner:	
Neighbor:	

House Information
(keys, locks, security system, flashlights, fire extinguisher, etc.)

Tools/Supplies Information
(mower, gas, trimmer, clippers, shovels, trash bags, cleaning supplies, etc.)

Tools/Supplies to Bring from Home
(gas, edger, clippers, safety glasses, etc.)

Instructions
(grass height, compost pile location, areas to shovel, where to put snow, etc.)

 Pro Mow Lawn Service
Rebecca Jones, 123 Address Drive, Dearborn, MI 48126
(313) 555-0139

Sample form: make yours fit your business!

Then write them down on a Customer Agreement form. You and the customer should each have a copy of the Agreement.

KNOW YOUR CUSTOMERS

Fill out a Customer Information form for each customer. Keep them in a folder with the Customer Agreements. Update the forms if anything changes.

HOW MUCH DID YOU MAKE?

Profit is the amount of money you have left after you subtract your expenses. If you are only charging for your time, it's all profit, right? Not so fast! Did you have to make flyers or business cards? Did you provide supplies to do the job?

Add up your expenses. Subtract the expenses from the amount you earned. The amount left over is your profit.

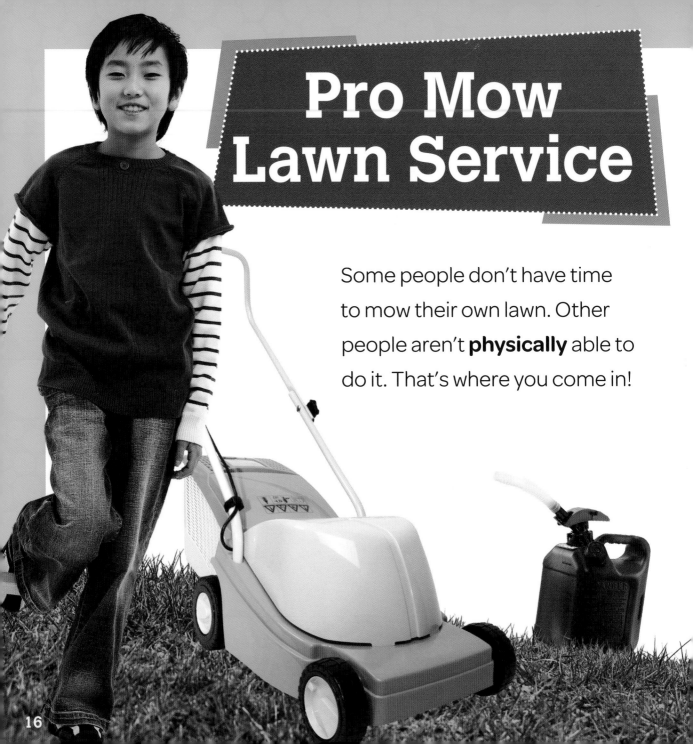

Pro Mow Lawn Service

Some people don't have time to mow their own lawn. Other people aren't **physically** able to do it. That's where you come in!

BEFORE YOU BEGIN

Look over a lawn before you agree to mow it. There may be hills that are hard for you to handle. Fill out a Customer Agreement form (see page 14). Write down all the details for the job.

Will you use your own mower? If you are using the customer's mower, have an adult show you how to use it first. A lawn mower can be a very **dangerous** machine. Be sure you are comfortable with the lawn mower before you use it.

If it's a gas mower, make sure there is enough gas and oil.

Get any special instructions on grass height, mowing pattern, and edge trimming.

What should you do with the clippings? Do you need to rake and bag them?

* Always have permission to use the lawn mower or edger.

* NEVER put your hands near the blades. If clumps of grass are stuck in the blades, turn off the mower. Try to loosen the clumps with a water hose. If that doesn't work, get an adult to help you.

* Wear closed shoes, not sandals! Use old shoes because they will get grass stains.

* Remove all **debris** from the lawn, such as sticks and toys.

* Wear safety glasses and earplugs.

* Don't mow when the grass is wet.

WHAT YOU'LL NEED

lawn mower (gas and oil if needed)

lawn edger

safety glasses

earplugs

old shoes and socks

Leaf the Raking to Me

It's fall, and there are leaves everywhere. When leaves pile up, they can ruin lawns. It's best to get them raked up. Raking leaves is hard **physical** work!

WHAT YOU'LL NEED

a leaf rake

work gloves

large leaf bags or a tarp

BEFORE YOU BEGIN

Talk with your customer about where and how to rake the leaves. Fill out a Customer Agreement form (see page 14). Write down all the details for the job.

Sometimes people keep leaves on top of garden areas through the winter.

Find out what to do with the leaves. Is there leaf pick-up? What are the rules for the leaf pick-up? Should the leaves be in bags or in a pile?

Is there a **compost** pile or bin for the leaves? You can rake the leaves onto a **tarp**. Then drag the tarp to the compost pile. Or you can use a wheelbarrow.

ON THE JOB

When you rake, keep working at a steady pace. Don't start off as fast as possible.

To keep from getting sore, try changing how you hold the rake. Switch from your right side to your left every half hour or so.

* Try using a snow shovel to put leaves into the bag.

* Wear work gloves to protect your hands.

* Try a metal and a plastic leaf rake to see which one works better for you.

SAVE TIME
If you charge by the job, make more money by saving time! Invest in a leaf bag holder.

Weeds Be Gone

Weeding is one of those tasks that many people dislike. It takes a lot of time and you have to be on your hands and knees in the dirt. There's no doubt that you can find plenty of customers wanting this service!

WHAT YOU'LL NEED
weeding tools
work gloves
trash bag or bucket

Before weeding, have your customer show you which plants are the weeds. Fill out a Customer Agreement form (see page 14). Write down all the details for the job.

Is there more than one garden area that needs weeding?

Find out where the garden tools are kept. Which tool does the customer suggest using?

Where should you put the weeds you've pulled? Does the customer have a **compost** bin? Or should you put the weeds in a trash bag?

Find out if you should water the garden when you're done weeding.

WELL DONE

If you do a good job, you're more likely to get hired again!

ON THE JOB

* Learn about common weeds in your area by searching online.

* Learn what poisonous plants look like and avoid them!

* Bring insect **repellent**, especially if the garden is in the shade!

* Wear old shoes and clothes that can get dirty.

* When you pull out a weed, try to get the whole root.

* Be careful if the weed is full of seeds. You don't want to plant more weeds!

Let It Snow Shoveling Service

If you live in a place where it snows, you know what a problem snow can be! Driveways and sidewalks need to be cleared. Slippery surfaces can be **dangerous**.

WHAT YOU'LL NEED

gloves

shovel

rock salt

ice chipper

BEFORE YOU BEGIN

Meet with your customer before starting so you know which areas you should shovel. Fill out a Customer Agreement form (see page 14). Write down all the details for the job.

Find out if the customer wants you to use rock salt or another ice melter.

Don't forget to shovel around the mailbox, trash cans, or other areas people need to get to.

You may be able to do part of the job before school. Then you can come back and finish after school. Ask the customer what area should be done first.

Make Your Own Ice Melt Bottle

Rinse out a plastic gallon jug, especially if it had milk in it. Decorate it with glitter glue. Use a funnel to fill the jug with an ice melting product.

LET IT SNOW

Ice Melt

* Before it snows, introduce yourself to your neighbors. Hand out your business card (see page 11). Ask people if they will hire you to shovel for them. Agree on a price beforehand. Then, when it snows, you will be ready to work.

* Be careful about the number of families you agree to shovel for. You don't want so many that you don't have time to do them all!

* Be careful when shoveling after multiple snowfalls. The lower layers freeze and harden. They can be slippery. This is where an ice chipper comes in handy.

* Have your own snow shovel. This is especially important if you are shoveling before people are awake. Try shovels of different sizes and weights to find the best one for you.

DO GOOD
Donate your time. **Volunteer** to shovel for those who can't afford to pay for it.

23

Clean Yard, Happy Yard

Some yards are a mess. Some messes are caused by nature, such as a tree that drops branches. Other messes, such as toys or tools left outside, are made by people. A messy yard can be **dangerous** to kids who are playing or someone trying to mow.

WHAT YOU'LL NEED

yard waste bags
work gloves
rake
twine

scissors
bucket
sponge
soap

BEFORE YOU BEGIN

Meet with the customer to find out what needs to be done. Fill out a Customer Agreement form (see page 14). Write down all the details for the job.

Does the customer have a yard waste pickup service? Should you tie branches together with twine?

Some bigger branches might need to be cut. Put them in a separate pile for an adult to cut with a saw.

Smaller twigs and branches can be put in yard waste bags. Where should you put the bags?

Is there lawn furniture or a swing set that needs washing?

Find out where any toys or tools should be put away.

ON THE JOB

✳ People may be **sensitive** about having messy yards. Be careful to ask nicely if you can clean up so you don't offend them.

✳ Use soap and water to clean plastic or metal lawn furniture. Ask the customer what to use to clean things made of cloth or wood.

✳ Look out for rusty metal and sharp objects such as nails or glass. Be careful not to cut yourself!

✳ Ask if you can put a sign in their yard while you are working. This may **attract** new customers!

GO GREEN
Is the family throwing out extra wood? Do you know someone who could use it? Recycle it!

Thirsty Plant Watering Service

Some plants and lawns require more than rain to keep them healthy. It's common for people to water the plants around their homes, especially if it hasn't rained in a while.

WHAT YOU'LL NEED

paper and pencil

hose

watering sprayer

watering can

sprinkler

BEFORE YOU BEGIN

Meet with the customer to find out what areas should be watered. Fill out a Customer Agreement form (see page 14). Write down all the details for the job.

Walk with the customer around the yard. Have the customer tell you what needs to be watered and how often.

Draw a map showing the areas you will need to water.

Find out where the hoses, sprinklers, sprayers, and outdoor faucets are.

ON THE JOB

* You may need to move sprinklers around the yard. Ask how long they should remain in each area before you need to move them.

* Early mornings are the best time to water. It's usually cooler and less windy in the morning. This keeps the sun from causing the water to **evaporate** as much.

* Find out if your town has rules about watering. Sometimes there are certain days you can't water lawns and gardens.

Learn about using a rain gauge. Then you'll know when lawns need to be watered!

Make Your Own Rain Gauge

Have an adult help you cut the top off of a 2-liter plastic bottle. Cut along the top of the widest part of the bottle. Cover the edges with tape. Make a mark about an inch from the bottom of the bottle. Write a zero next to the mark. Lay the end of a ruler at the zero mark. Mark off inches and half inches up the side of the bottle. Put a layer of pebbles in the bottom of the bottle. Add water up to the zero mark. Put the top of the bottle in upside down, so it funnels water into the bottom. Place the rain gauge in an open area outside.

27

For the Birds

People get a lot of pleasure watching the birds that visit their yards. No matter where you live, you can **attract** birds with a bird feeder or a birdbath!

stepladder
scrub brush
water
trash bag

Meet with the customer to find out where the bird feeder and birdbath are. Fill out a Customer Agreement form (see page 14). Write down all the details for the job.

Will you supply the bird seed, or will the customer?

It is important to clean the bird feeder to keep the seeds from getting moldy.

If the bird feeder is high up, use a stepladder. Never use a regular ladder by yourself.

Clean up the seed shells that fall on the ground. Put them in a trash bag.

Clean birdbaths and fill them with fresh water every few days.

ON THE JOB

* There is a lot of information about the placement, cleaning, and maintenance of bird feeders. Spend some time at the library or online learning about feeding birds.

* Other people might get a bird feeder if they know you can take care of it for them. You could put a notice up at locations that sell bird food.

* Offer to help customers learn about the birds in your area. Find out what kind of feeders and food will **attract** birds to their yards. You could see what's for sale at nearby bird supply stores.

* Make sure birdbaths are far from places cats can hide! They love to jump out and catch wet birds.

Make a Pinecone Bird Feeder

Tie a piece of string or ribbon to the bottom of the pinecone. Spread peanut butter all over the pinecone. Cover the peanut butter with bird seed. Hang the pinecone in a tree for the birds.

29

Tips for Success

Success isn't measured just by how much money you make. How you look and behave is also important.

BE ON TIME

Show that you are responsible and follow through on your agreements.

BE POLITE

This means that you need to respect your customer. Do not interrupt. Ask any questions politely. Be respectful even if you don't agree with someone.

DRESS FOR THE JOB

Be neat and clean, even if it's a dirty job! Wear the right clothing for the job.

BE ON THE SAFE SIDE

Follow safety instructions. Review tool or equipment safety before you start a job. Never try to use a tool or machine that you are not familiar with. Always have **emergency** contact information.

ALWAYS COMPLETE THE JOB

Remember the agreement you made? You need to follow through and do everything you agreed to do. Put away all tools and supplies you use. If you are messy or don't finish a job, you probably won't be hired again!

THIS IS JUST THE BEGINNING

Okay, it is the end of the book. But, it is just the beginning for you! This book has provided information about some ways to make money. Now decide what might work for you. Talk it over with your parents. And don't forget to have fun!

Glossary

attract – to cause someone or something to come near.

compost – a mixture of decaying organic substances used for fertilizing soil.

dangerous – able or likely to cause harm or injury.

debris – the remains of something after it has been destroyed.

discouraged – feeling that you can't do something, or that something isn't worth trying.

emergency – a sudden, unexpected, dangerous situation that requires immediate attention.

evaporate – to change from a liquid into a gas.

guardian – the person who, by law, cares for a minor.

master – an original copy that is reproduced to make more of the same thing.

material – the substance something is made of, such as metal, fabric, or plastic.

physical – having to do with the body.

repellent – something that keeps other things from coming close.

sensitive – embarrassed or ashamed.

tarp – short for tarpaulin. A large piece of material, such as canvas or plastic.

volunteer – to offer to do a job, most often without pay.

Index

Abilities and interests (and types of work done), 6, 7
Advertising. *See* Business cards; Flyers

Bird feeding/watering, 28–29
Business cards, 10–11

Charging (for work), 14, 19, 23
Cleaning yards, 24–25
Clothing (for work), 9, 17, 19, 21, 30
Costs (of starting/doing work), 7, 14, 15
Customer Agreement form, 14–15, 17, 19, 21, 23, 25, 27, 29, 30
Customer Information form, 8, 15
Customers
    expectations of, 8, 14–15, 30
    getting, 6, 10–13, 23, 25
    information about, 8, 15
    treatment of, 25, 30

Disposing (of materials), 17, 19, 21, 25
Donating money, 5

Expenses (of work), 15. *See also* Costs

Feeding/Watering birds, 28–29
Fees (for work). *See* Charging
Flyers, 12–13
Friends (working with), 7, 8

Garden watering, 21, 26–27
Garden weeding, 20–21
Getting customers, 6, 10–13, 23, 25
Goal setting (for work), 7

Ice melt bottle, 23
Insect repellent, 21
Investing money, 5

Ladders (safe use of), 29
Lawn mowing, 16–17
Lawn watering, 26–27
Laws (about kids working), 6
Leaf raking, 18–19
Location (of work), 6, 8, 9

Money
    deciding what to charge, 14, 19, 23
    earning, 4, 15
    uses of, 5
Mowing lawns, 16–17

Parents
    getting advice/permission from, 5, 7, 8, 9, 10, 12, 17
    providing information to, 8, 9
Physical fitness (and work), 9, 19
Pinecone bird feeder, 29
Planning (of work), 6–7, 17, 19, 21, 23, 25, 27, 29
Plant watering, 21, 26–27
Poisonous plants, 9, 21
Profits (from work), 15
Pulling weeds, 20–21

Quality (of work done), 4, 30

Rain gauge, 27
Raking leaves, 18–19
Reasons (for working), 4
Recycling, 25. *See also* Disposing

Safety
    dangerous materials/surfaces, 23, 25
    guidelines, 9, 30
    poisonous plants, 9, 21
    tool use, 9, 17, 29
Saving money, 5
Schedule/Time (of work), 8, 9, 23, 27, 30

School (and work), 7, 23
Snow shoveling, 22–23
Spending money, 5

Tools and supplies (for work)
    cost of, 14, 15
    identification of, 7, 17, 18, 20, 21, 22, 23, 24, 26, 28
    putting away, 30
    safe use of, 9, 17, 29
Transportation (to/from work), 8

Volunteering, 4, 23

Watering/Feeding birds, 28–29
Watering gardens/plants/lawns, 21, 26–27
Weeding, 20–21

Yard cleanup, 24–25